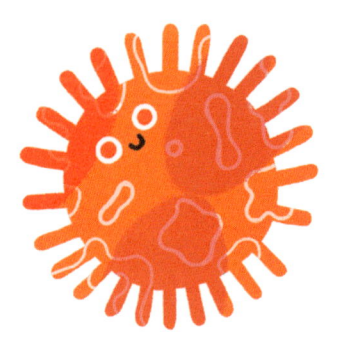

For Harry – E.G

For my parents – M.L

First published in Great Britain in 2021 by Wren & Rook

Text copyright © Emily Grossman, 2021
Illustration copyright © Maggie Li, 2021

The right of Emily Grossman and Maggie Li to be identified as author and illustrator respectively of this work has been asserted by them in accordance with the Copyright, Designs and Patents Act 1988.

All rights reserved.

HB ISBN: 978 1 5263 6356 5
PB ISBN: 978 1 5263 6357 2
E-book ISBN: 978 1 5263 6370 1

1 3 5 7 9 10 8 6 4 2

Wren & Rook
An imprint of
Hachette Children's Group
Part of Hodder & Stoughton
Carmelite House
50 Victoria Embankment
London EC4Y 0DZ

An Hachette UK Company
www.hachette.co.uk
www.hachettechildrens.co.uk

Publishing Director: Debbie Foy
Editor: Phoebe Jascourt
Art Director: Laura Hambleton

Printed in China

Every effort has been made to clear copyright. Should there be any inadvertent omission, please apply to the publisher for rectification.

The website addresses (URLs) included in this book were valid at the time of going to press. However, it is possible that contents or addresses may have changed since the publication of this book. No responsibility for any such changes can be accepted by either the author or the publisher.

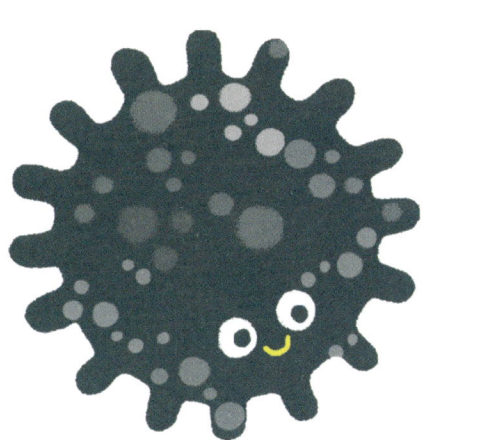

Meet the MICROBES!

DR EMILY GROSSMAN

Illustrated by MAGGIE LI

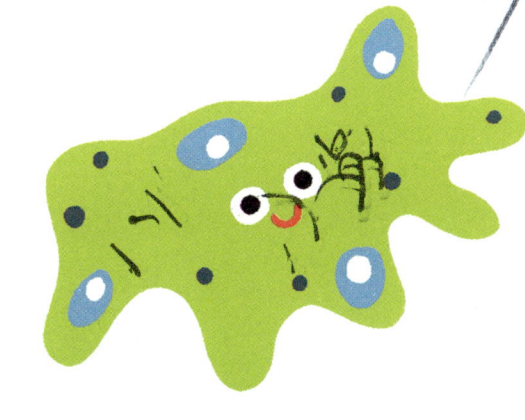

wren &rook

Welcome to the wonderful world of microbes!

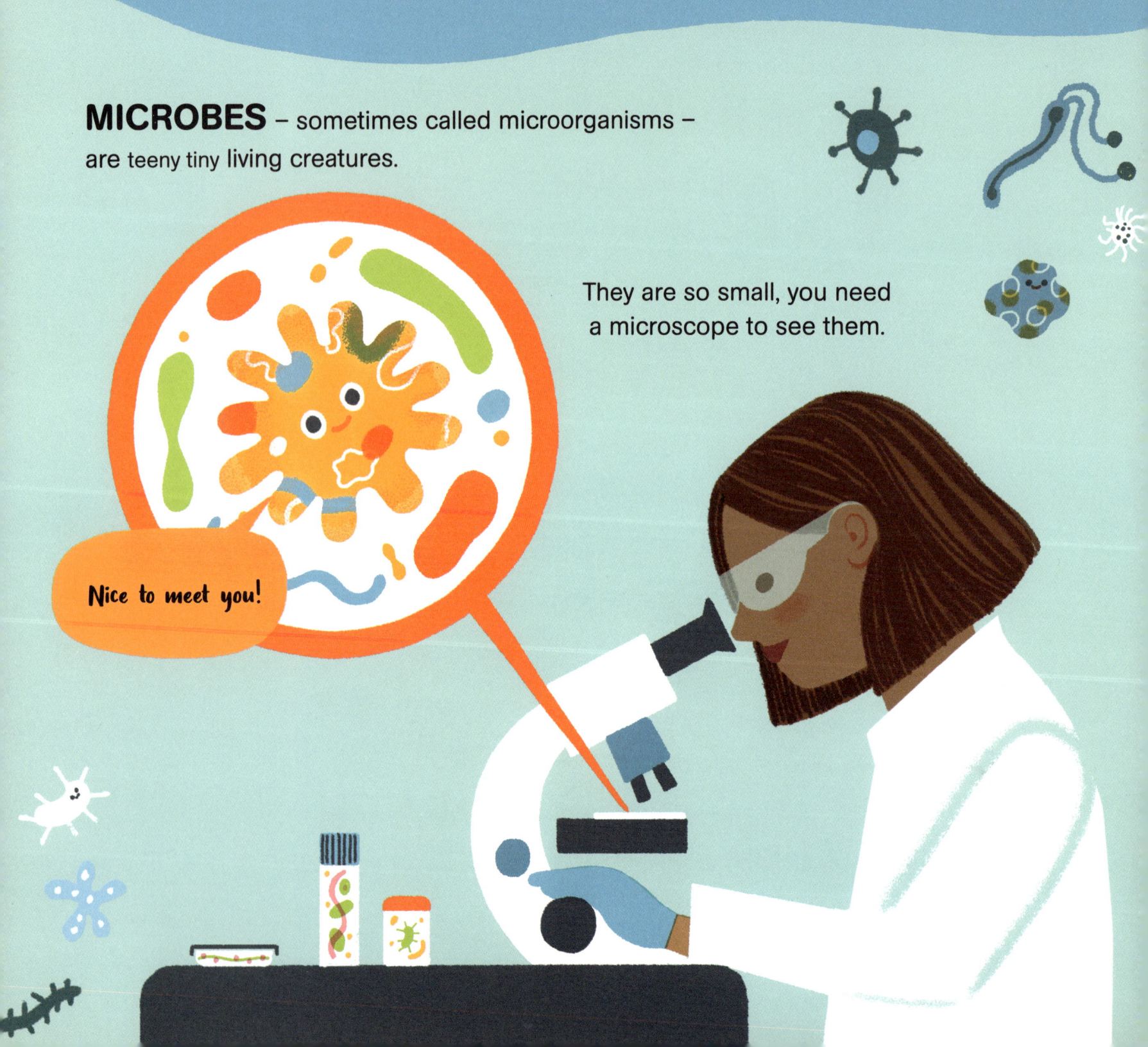

MICROBES – sometimes called microorganisms – are teeny tiny living creatures.

They are so small, you need a microscope to see them.

Nice to meet you!

More than **ONE BILLION** microbes could fit on this full stop.

This one here!

Some microbes are **BAD**...

I'll save you!

... but most of them are **GOOD**.

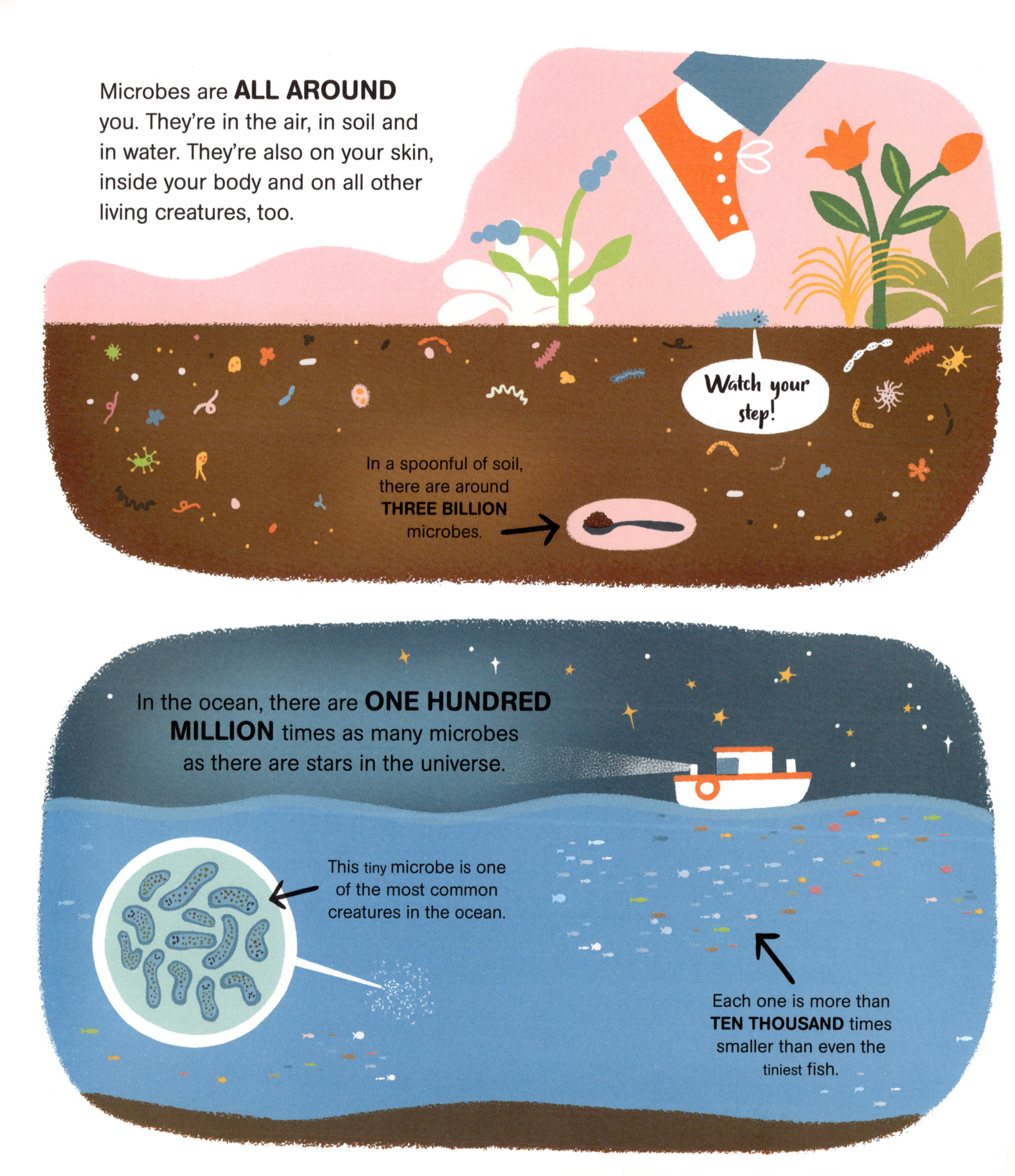

Microbes are **ALL AROUND** you. They're in the air, in soil and in water. They're also on your skin, inside your body and on all other living creatures, too.

Watch your step!

In a spoonful of soil, there are around **THREE BILLION** microbes.

In the ocean, there are **ONE HUNDRED MILLION** times as many microbes as there are stars in the universe.

This tiny microbe is one of the most common creatures in the ocean.

Each one is more than **TEN THOUSAND** times smaller than even the tiniest fish.

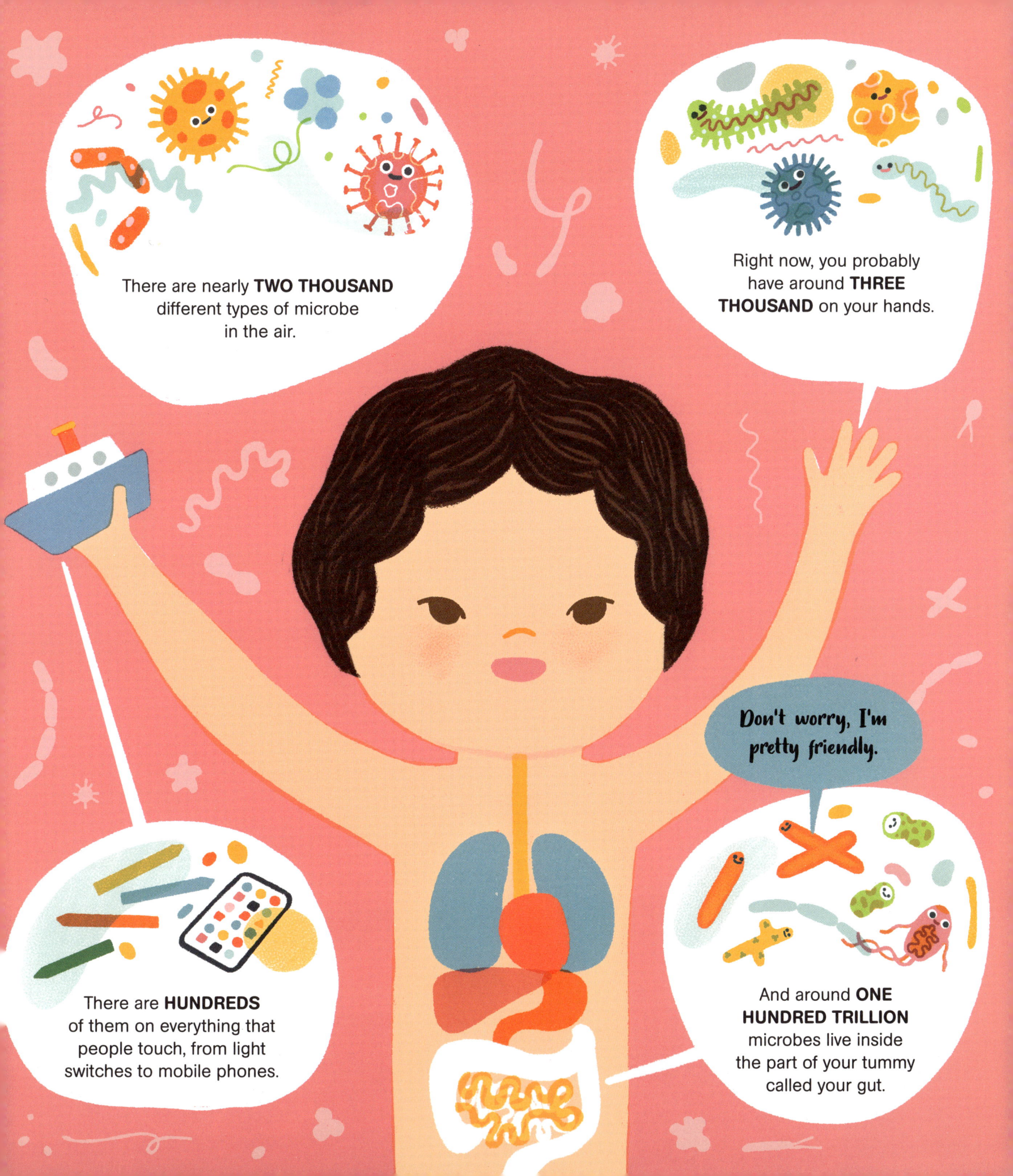

There are nearly **TWO THOUSAND** different types of microbe in the air.

Right now, you probably have around **THREE THOUSAND** on your hands.

Don't worry, I'm pretty friendly.

There are **HUNDREDS** of them on everything that people touch, from light switches to mobile phones.

And around **ONE HUNDRED TRILLION** microbes live inside the part of your tummy called your gut.

In fact, microbes can survive in very **EXTREME** places...

"Where did I put my gloves?"

In the frosty depths of Antarctica,

"But I'm scared of the dark!"

inside rocks below the Earth's surface,

"I'm stuck in the mud!"

in mud at the bottom of the sea,

"Toasty."

in the scalding heat of hot springs,

"Peace and quiet at last!"

in the airless vacuum of outer space,

"Brr!"

and in the soil of the coldest, driest valleys on Earth.

And they can live for **MILLIONS** of years!

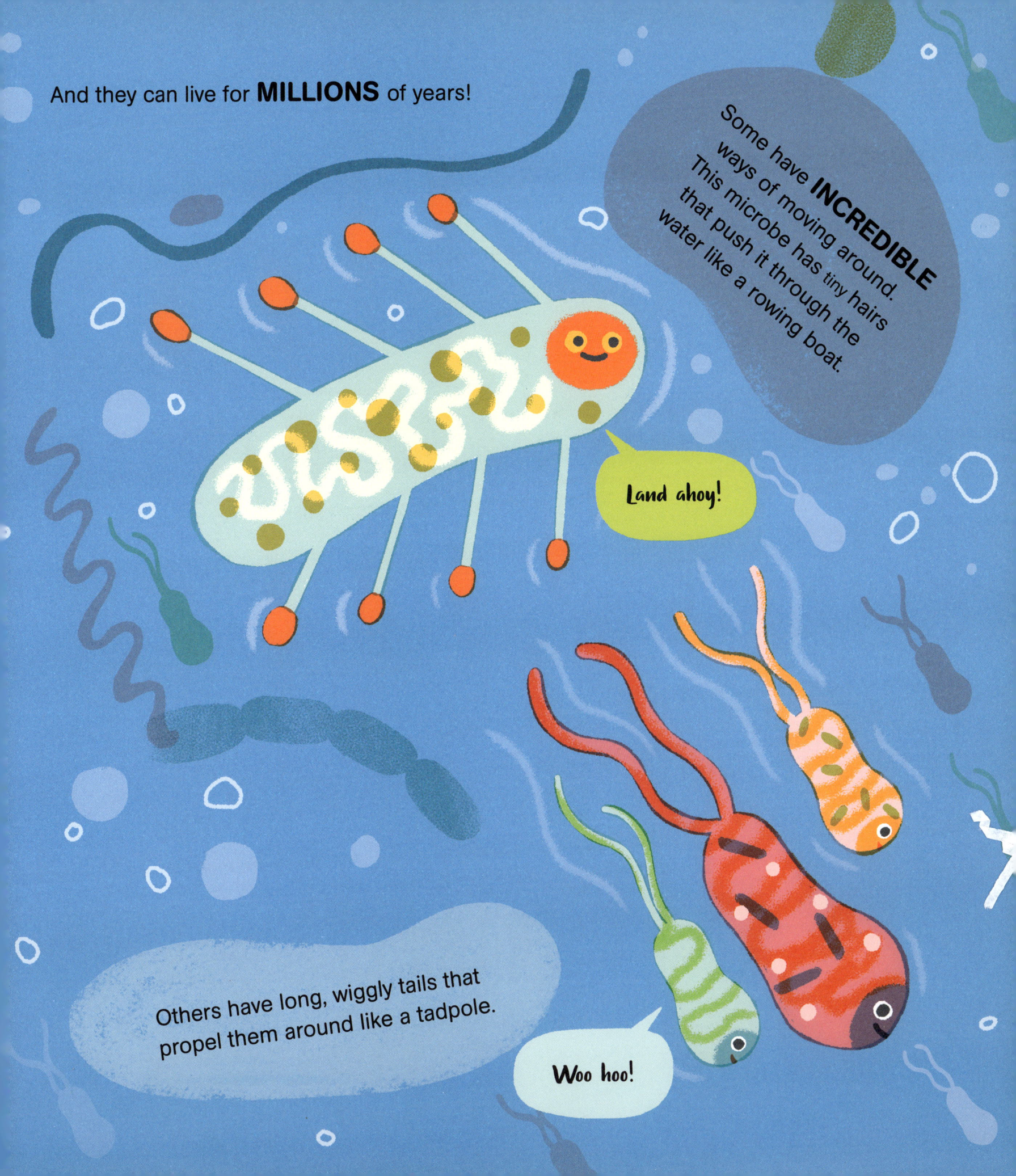

Some have **INCREDIBLE** ways of moving around. This microbe has tiny hairs that push it through the water like a rowing boat.

Land ahoy!

Others have long, wiggly tails that propel them around like a tadpole.

Woo hoo!

The most common types of microbe are **BACTERIA, VIRUSES** and **FUNGI**.

rods, spirals and spheres.

BACTERIA come in lots of different shapes and sizes, such as...

All living things are made up of cells. Bacteria have just one cell, but your body has about **THIRTY TRILLION**!

I can get along just fine on my own, thank you.

Bacteria were one of the earliest life forms to appear on Earth. Today you can find them pretty much anywhere.

Just like **YOU**, bacteria need food to survive. Some make their own food from sunlight. Others take in food from what's around them. They don't have mouths, so they just suck in what they need through the outside of their cell.

They feed off all sorts of things, from dead or living creatures to rocks and soil.

Unlike most other living creatures, bacteria don't always need oxygen to survive. That's why they can live in such **CRAZY** places.

WANTED, DEAD OR ALIVE

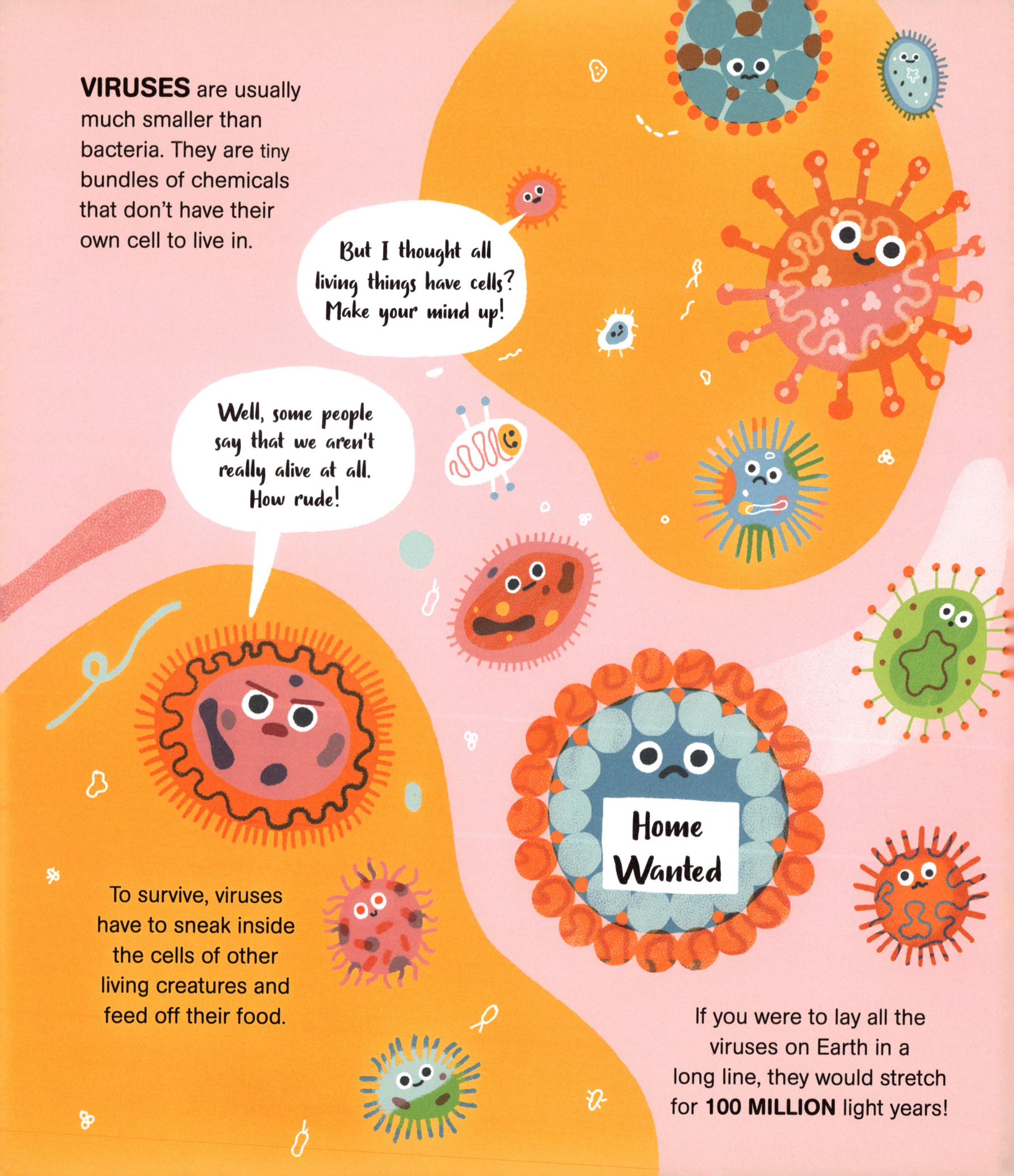

VIRUSES are usually much smaller than bacteria. They are tiny bundles of chemicals that don't have their own cell to live in.

But I thought all living things have cells? Make your mind up!

Well, some people say that we aren't really alive at all. How rude!

To survive, viruses have to sneak inside the cells of other living creatures and feed off their food.

Home Wanted

If you were to lay all the viruses on Earth in a long line, they would stretch for **100 MILLION** light years!

FUNGI are a group of living organisms that feast on dead and decaying plants and animals.

I'm a **HUMONGOUS** fungus.

MOULD is a type of fungus. It can be black, white, orange, green or even purple. It often looks fluffy when a patch forms.

Not all fungi are small enough to be microbes.

Yum ... my favourite!

One of the most **AMAZING** things about some microbes is just how quickly they can make copies of themselves.

Bacteria

The microbe simply grows a bit, then splits in two. Then each new microbe grows a bit more and splits in two again.

As long as they have plenty of food, some microbes can grow and split every 20 minutes.

When viruses make copies of themselves, they wriggle their way inside another living cell. Here, they make lots of new virus particles... that then burst out!

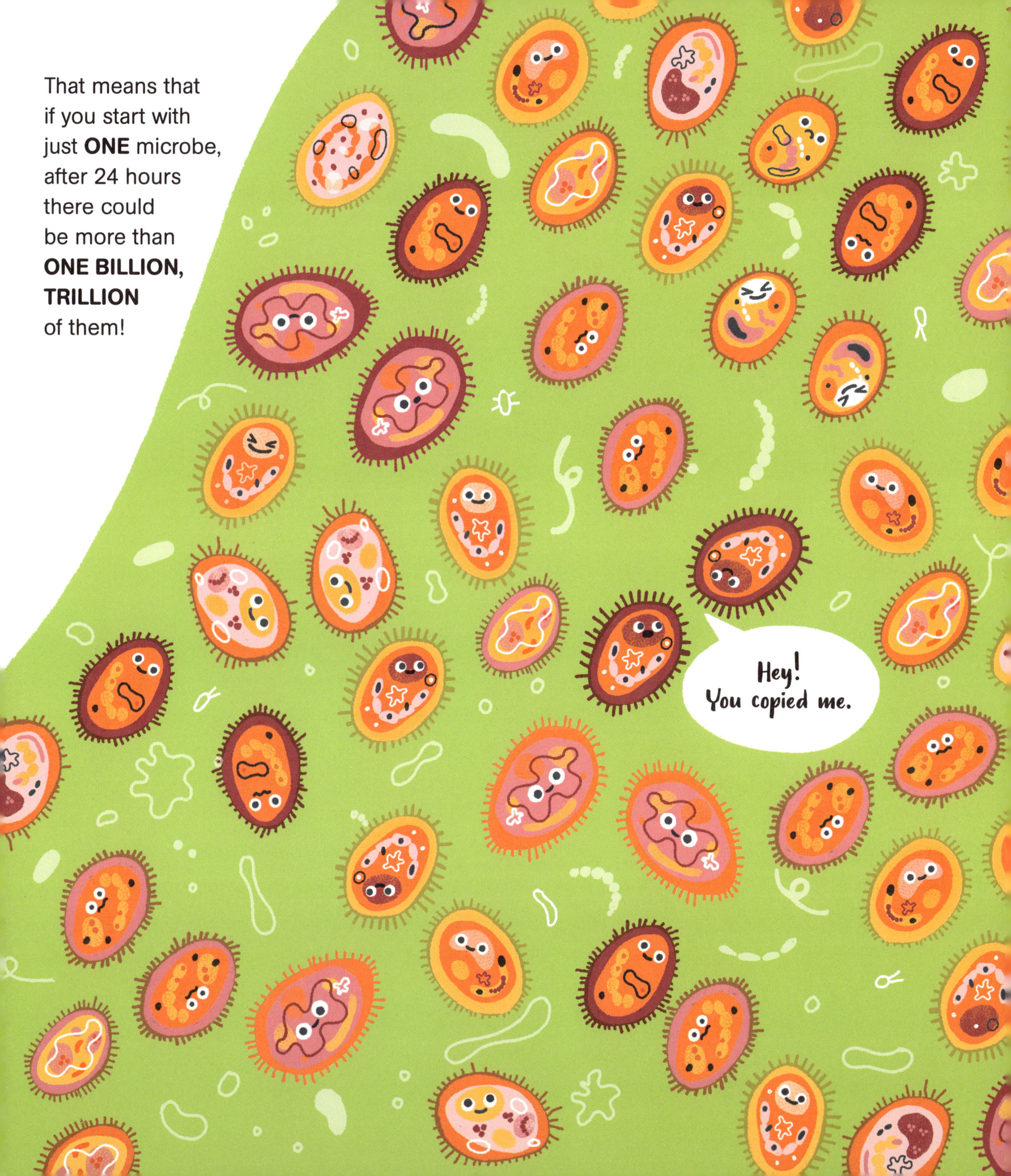

That means that if you start with just **ONE** microbe, after 24 hours there could be more than **ONE BILLION, TRILLION** of them!

Hey! You copied me.

Most microbes are harmless to us.
In fact, many are very helpful.

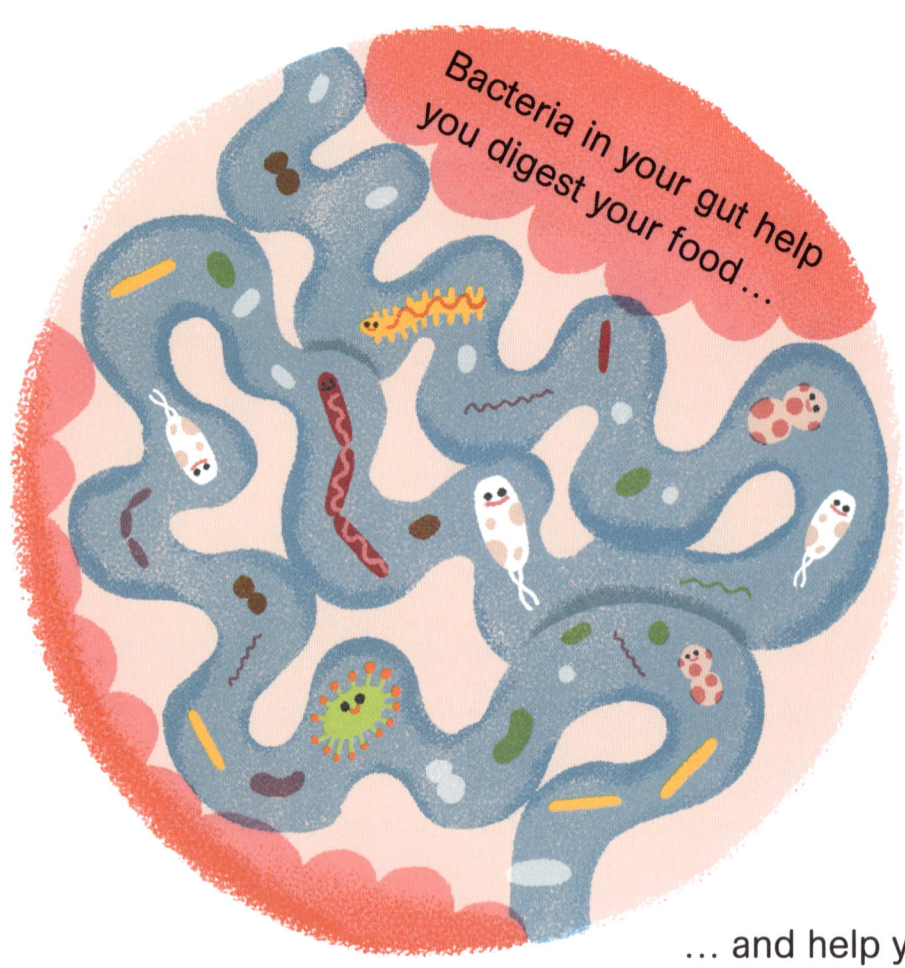

Bacteria in your gut help you digest your food...

... and help your body fight off any harmful microbes that you might have swallowed.

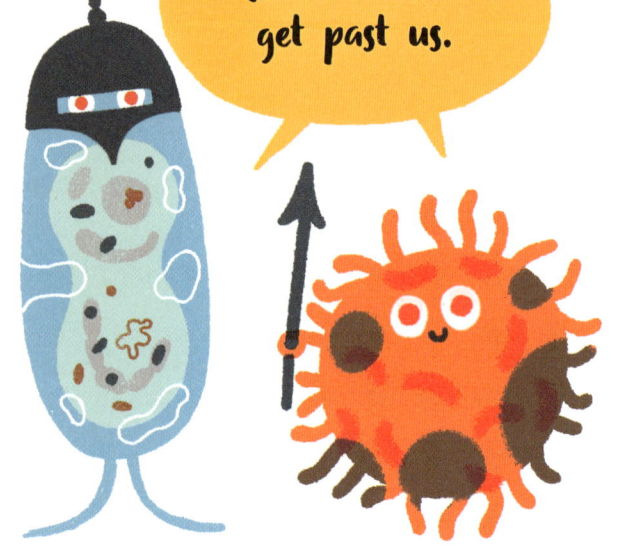

You'll have to get past us.

Microbes also help to keep the planet clean and healthy. Microbes living in the soil break down anything that has died, including wood and leaves, to make sure that **IMPORTANT** nutrients are returned to the soil. This helps plants grow.

In fact, without all these microbes, our planet would be **COVERED** with rubbish!

Microbes also help to make some of the **DELICIOUS** food that we eat.

Hiccup!

YEAST microbes feed off sugars in dough. They produce bubbles of gas that cause the dough to rise, forming bread.

If there are any microbes on a baker's hands, they sometimes end up in the dough too, which can change the entire flavour of the bread!

Yeast microbes also feed off sugars in sweet drinks. The bubbles of gas they produce turn the drink fizzy.

Pardon me!

You can also eat microbes themselves...

Bacteria help us turn milk into cheese and yoghurt.

...you can spread yeast on your toast,

or make **TASTY** vegetarian dishes from a special type of fungus.

Microbes have been very useful to scientists throughout history, and they still are today.

Without mould, Alexander Fleming would never have discovered the first antibiotic, a special medicine called penicillin, which has saved **MILLIONS** of lives.

Scientists also use microbes to create important vaccines that stop people from getting sick with certain diseases, such as measles and COVID-19.

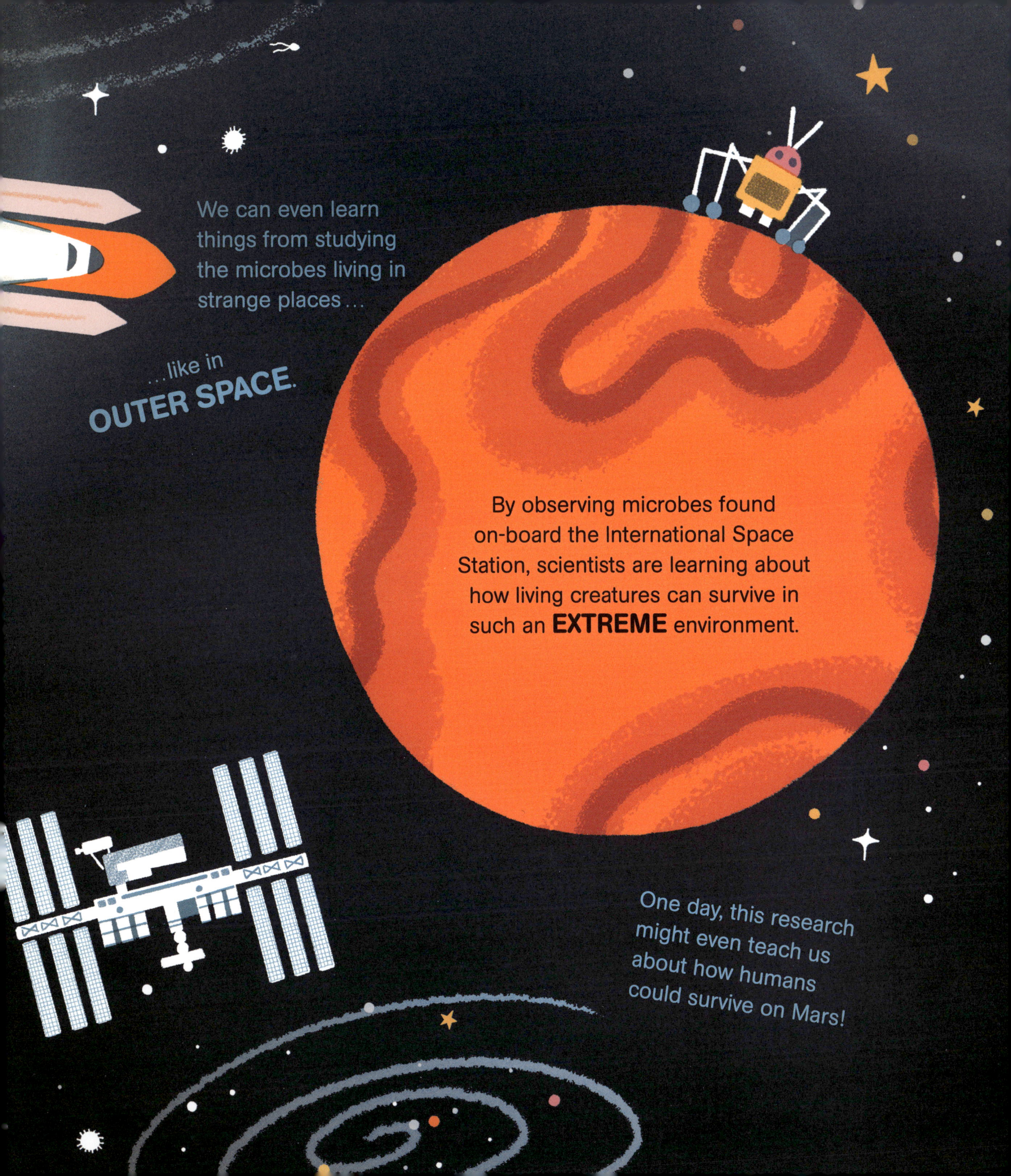

We can even learn things from studying the microbes living in strange places...

...like in
OUTER SPACE.

By observing microbes found on-board the International Space Station, scientists are learning about how living creatures can survive in such an **EXTREME** environment.

One day, this research might even teach us about how humans could survive on Mars!

While more than 99% of all types of microbe on the planet are harmless, there are a small few that can make you sick.

These microbes are called pathogens, although most people know them as **GERMS**.

The good news is that your body has lots of clever ways to protect you from them.

TEARS contain chemicals that kill germs that sneak into your eyes.

TINY HAIRS AND SNOT inside your nose trap any germs that you breathe in. The germs then either shoot out when you blow your nose, or get swallowed down into your tummy.

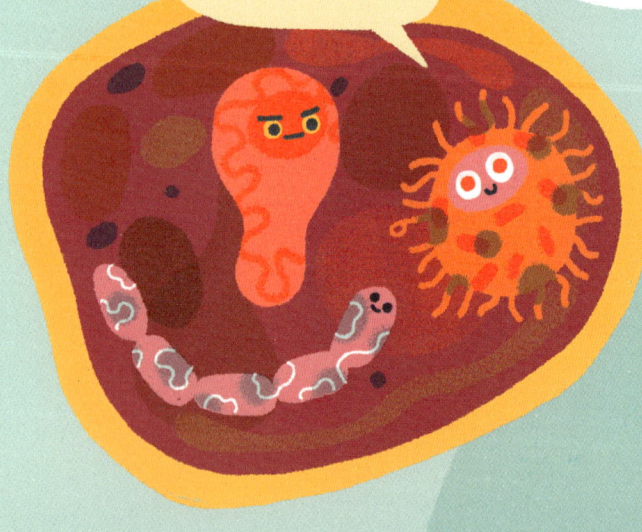

Let us in!

YOUR SKIN is a protective layer around your body. If you get a cut, a scab usually forms, which stops germs from coming in.

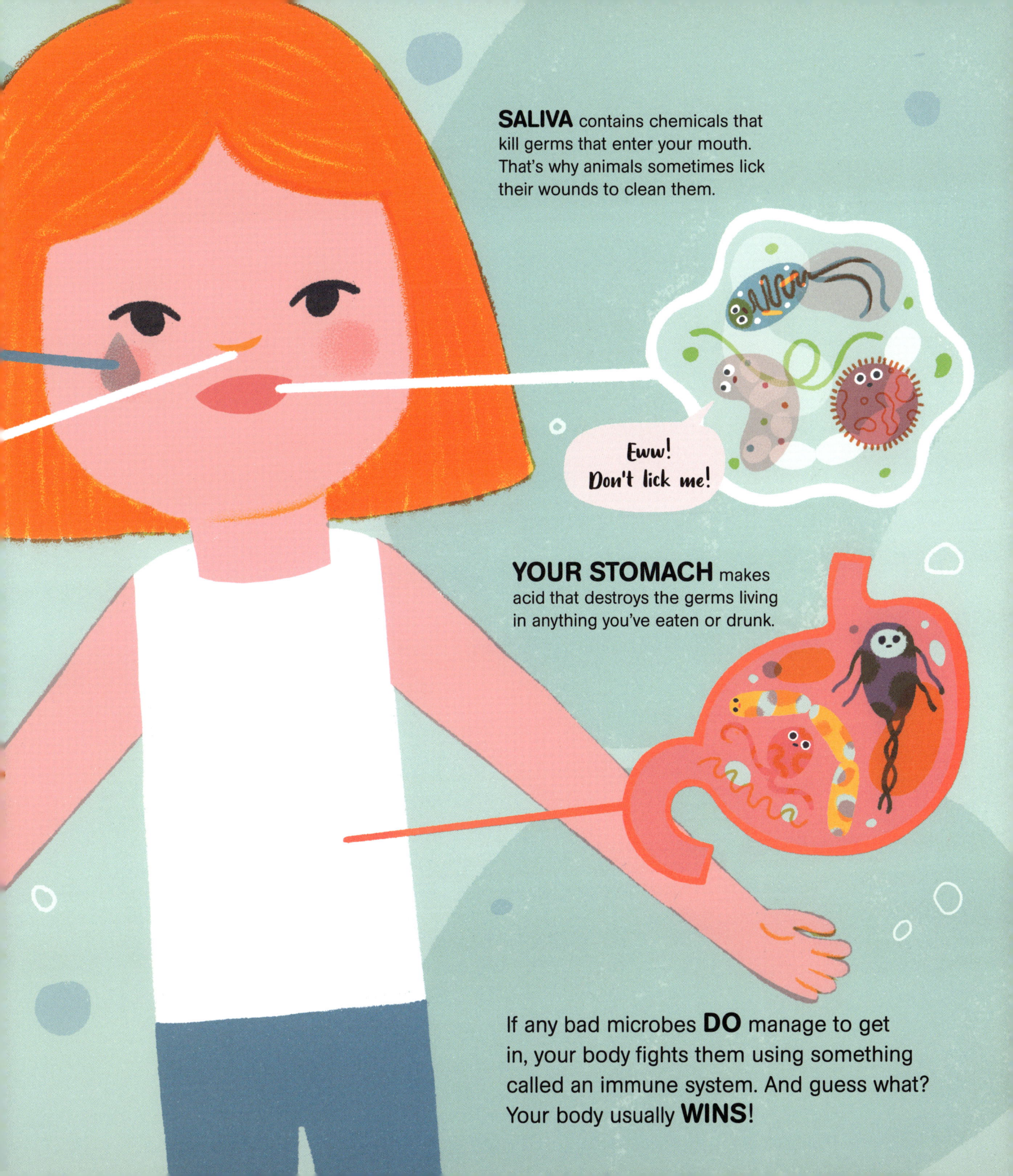

SALIVA contains chemicals that kill germs that enter your mouth. That's why animals sometimes lick their wounds to clean them.

Eww! Don't lick me!

YOUR STOMACH makes acid that destroys the germs living in anything you've eaten or drunk.

If any bad microbes **DO** manage to get in, your body fights them using something called an immune system. And guess what? Your body usually **WINS**!

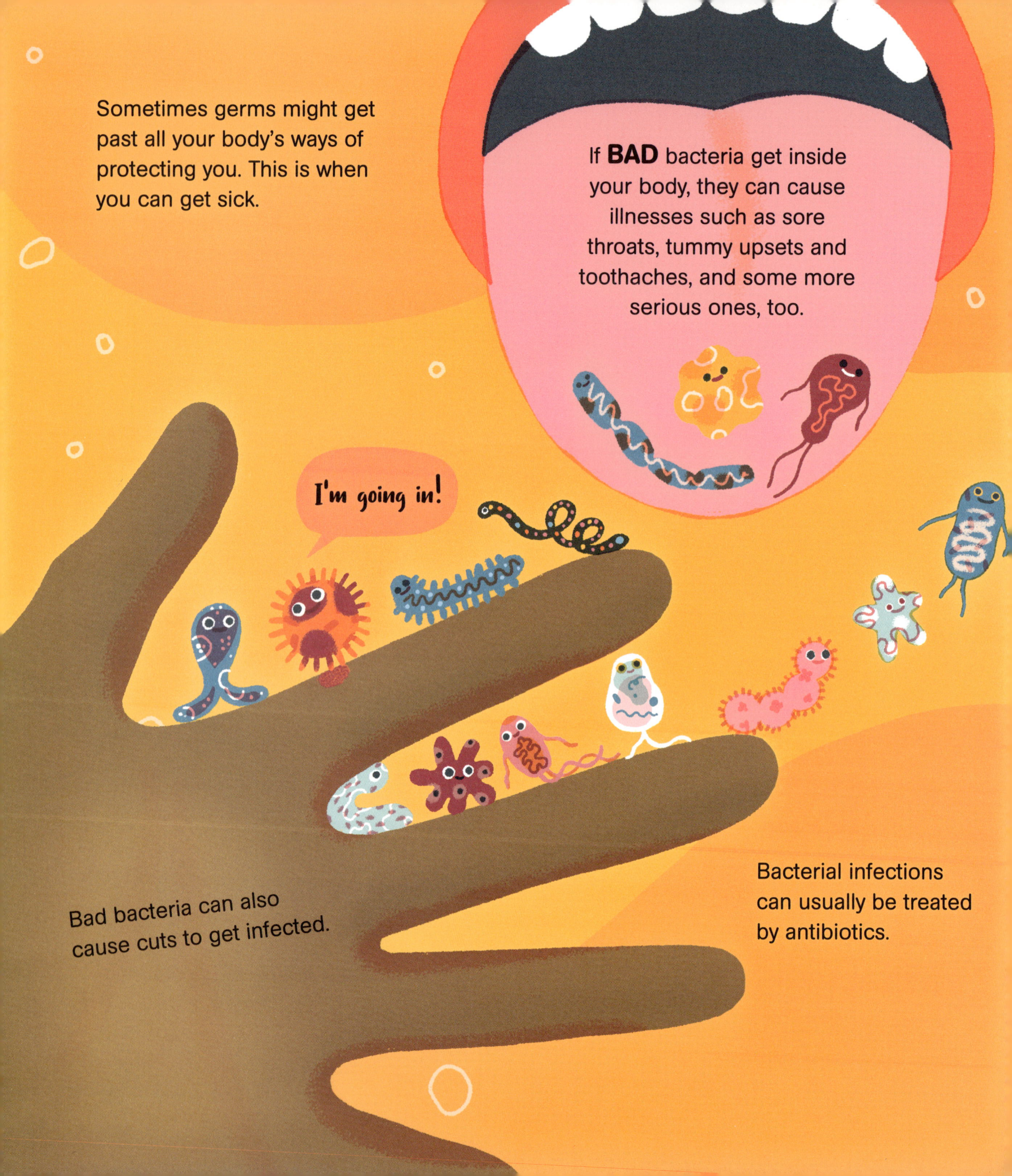

Sometimes germs might get past all your body's ways of protecting you. This is when you can get sick.

If **BAD** bacteria get inside your body, they can cause illnesses such as sore throats, tummy upsets and toothaches, and some more serious ones, too.

I'm going in!

Bad bacteria can also cause cuts to get infected.

Bacterial infections can usually be treated by antibiotics.

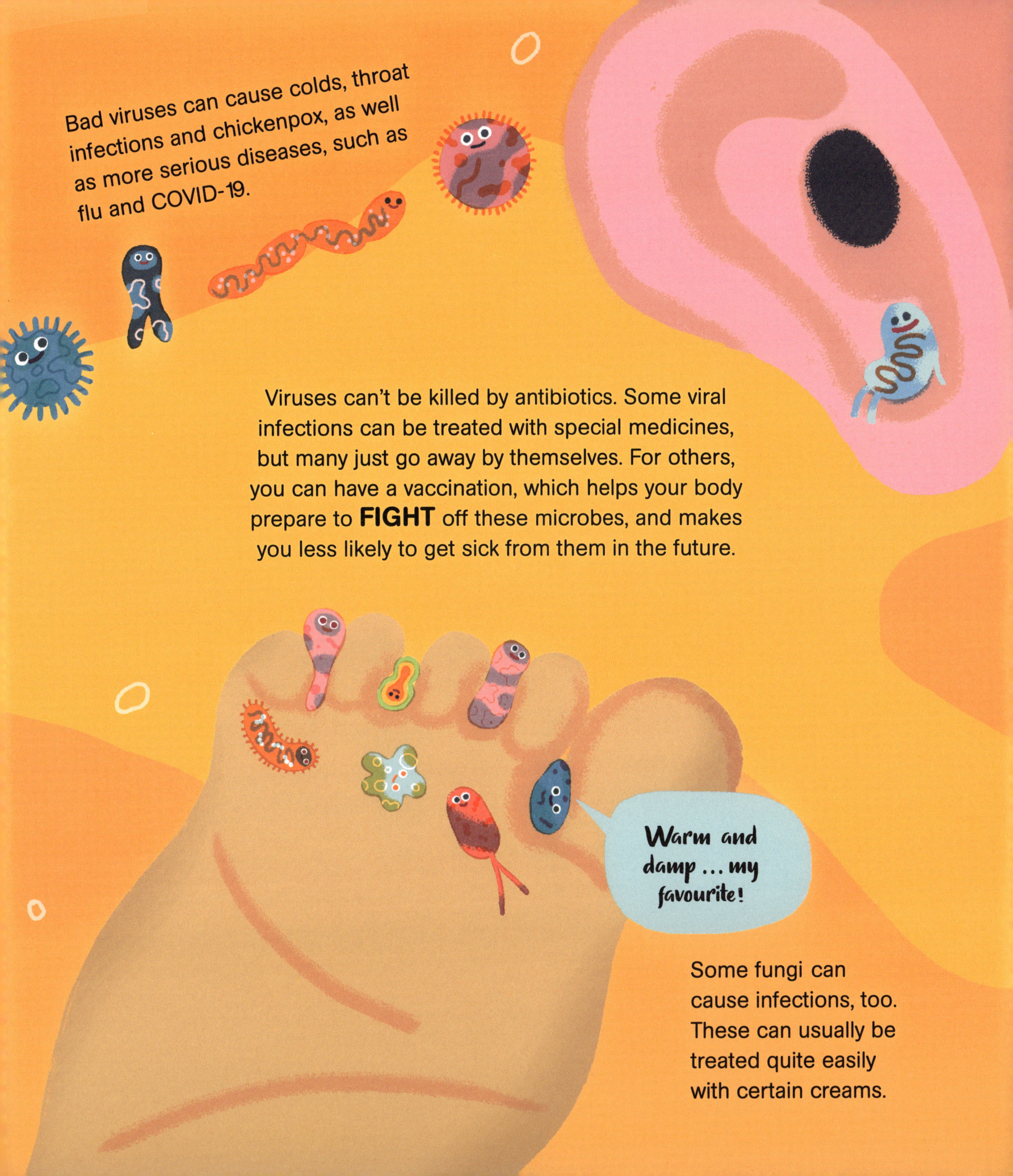

Bad viruses can cause colds, throat infections and chickenpox, as well as more serious diseases, such as flu and COVID-19.

Viruses can't be killed by antibiotics. Some viral infections can be treated with special medicines, but many just go away by themselves. For others, you can have a vaccination, which helps your body prepare to **FIGHT** off these microbes, and makes you less likely to get sick from them in the future.

Warm and damp... my favourite!

Some fungi can cause infections, too. These can usually be treated quite easily with certain creams.

Diseases caused by microbes are infectious, which means that the germs can get passed from person to person.

But **DON'T WORRY!** There are some easy ways to protect yourself.

Weeee!

Look out, here I come!

When someone coughs, sneezes or breathes out, germs from their body enter the air. Other people can then breathe them in.

So it's best to keep a few metres away from someone who is unwell, and not share food or drinks with them.

Germs can also be passed onto objects when someone touches them. So it's **IMPORTANT** to wash your hands after handling things that lots of other people might have touched.

Germs like to hang around on toilets, animals and uncooked meat. So wash your hands if you go near any of these things, too.

In some countries, germs are carried by mosquitos. Using mosquito repellent and sleeping under a net can keep you **SAFE** from them.

If you get a cut or a graze, wash it with water to help stop it from getting infected.

If **YOU** are feeling unwell, you could pass germs to other people around you. But there are lots of ways that you can protect others so they don't get sick, too.

Run!

COVER your nose and mouth with your arm, when you cough or sneeze.

If you can get one in time, it's even better to **CATCH** your sneeze in a tissue.

And try to keep a few metres away from other people, especially those who might get sick easily, such as elderly people.

Wash your hands regularly, especially after going to the toilet. Make sure you do this before touching your face!

Use lots of soap to get all the germs off. Then, keep washing for as long as it takes to sing **Happy Birthday** twice.

I'm here to help!

But most importantly… **DON'T BE AFRAID!** Although some microbes can make you sick, most of them are actually doing incredibly **IMPORTANT** things for us and the Earth.

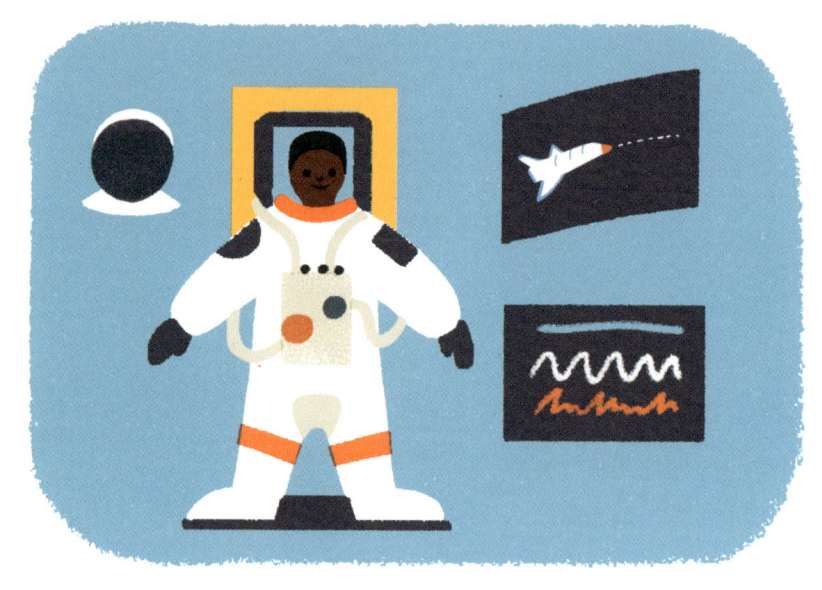

In the **FUTURE**, microbes could help us protect the planet. Some could break down rubbish and turn it into energy that could power our homes.

They could even produce enough energy to power **SPACE MISSIONS**!

So while it's good to remember how to protect ourselves from the bad microbes, we shouldn't be afraid of these teeny tiny creatures.

Let's be friends!

Happy to help!

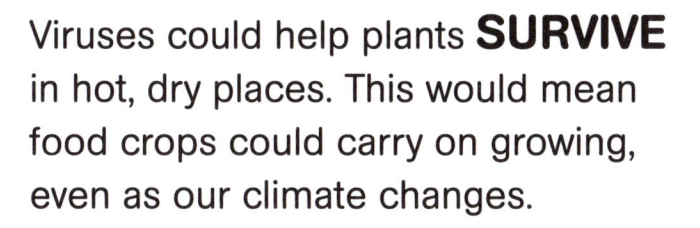

Viruses could help plants **SURVIVE** in hot, dry places. This would mean food crops could carry on growing, even as our climate changes.

Soon we may be able to make **HUGE** amounts of food from microbes. Scientists are creating a special flour, made using bacteria, which could feed millions of people in an eco-friendly way.

See, I'm not so scary after all.

Does that mean it's the end of the book?

Especially as so many are doing **AMAZING** things to keep us and our planet happy and healthy.

Isn't the world of microbes really rather **INCREDIBLE?**

Glossary

Antibiotics
Special medicines that help your body fight off bacterial infections. It's very important to finish your course of antibiotics, even if you start to feel better, to keep the infection from returning.

Cells
The building blocks of all living things, like how bricks are the building blocks of a house.

Chickenpox
A common viral infection that causes an itchy, spotty rash and can be spread by being in the same room as someone who has it. It usually gets better on its own.

Climate
The types of weather in an area. Our climate is changing due to global warming.

COVID-19
An infection caused by a virus called coronavirus, which causes a cough, high temperature and often a change to your sense of smell or taste. It is spread very easily by coming close to people who have it or touching things that they have touched. It can often get better on its own, especially in young people, but sometimes it can make people very sick and they have to go to hospital. Having a vaccination can stop you from getting it and may also help stop it from spreading.

Eco-friendly
Things that we can do to help look after our planet and all the creatures that live on it, such as buying less stuff and looking after our wildlife.

Flu
A common viral infection that can feel like a bad cold but can sometimes make people very ill. It can easily spread to others. It usually gets better on its own, but some people prefer to have a vaccination every year to stop them from getting it.

Fossil fuels
Fuels such as coal, oil and natural gas that were formed millions of years ago. They are burnt today to release energy to power cars, factories and our homes.

Global warming
The Earth is getting hotter because of chemicals that are being added to our atmosphere, such as carbon dioxide from the burning of fossil fuels and methane from cow burps. Global warming is causing changes to our weather, melting ice and raising sea levels.

Immune system
The cells in your body that fight off the germs that get inside.

Infectious disease
A disease that can be passed from one person to another.

Light year
The distance that you would travel if you moved at the speed of light for one year. (The actual distance is nine trillion kilometres – that's a nine with twelve zeros after it!)

Measles
A viral infection that causes a cold and a red blotchy rash, and can easily be spread by coughs and sneezes. It usually gets better on its own but it can make some people very sick. Thankfully, people hardly ever get measles any more as most children are given a vaccination against it.

Microscope
A piece of equipment that scientists look through to see really small things.

Mosquito repellent
A cream or liquid that can be put on your skin or your clothes to help stop mosquitos and other insects from landing on you and biting you.

Nutrients
Chemicals that living creatures need in order to survive and grow.

Penicillin
The first antibiotic to be discovered. It is used to treat bacterial infections, such as ear, mouth or throat infections.

Scab
A hard, dry layer of blood that forms over a cut to help it heal and to stop germs from getting in.

Stomach acid
The chemical in your tummy that helps to kill any germs in your food.

Vaccination
An injection containing special chemicals that prepare your body's immune system to fight off an infection in the future.

WOW... so many big words!

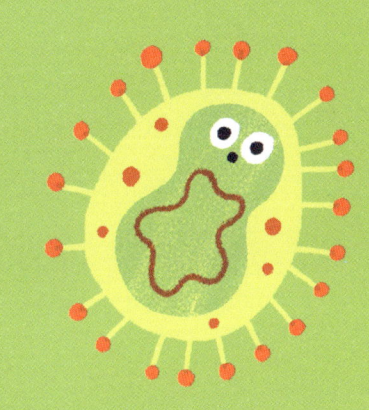